Claire Rayner
The Bodook

Introduction by Dr Hugh Jolly
Illustrated by Tony King

Hippo

Contents

Introduction

It needs a great deal of understanding of children and a lot of genius to write simply about something as complicated as their bodies, and to do so in such a way that their interest is maintained. Claire Rayner, Tony King with his superb illustrations, and her publishers have achieved this and made it all fun as well as being understandable and instructive.
I have no doubt that children will enjoy the book if their parents do. Parents create the atmosphere so that a child either enjoys a book like this or thinks it 'cissy'. This book is highly technical but I do not think that children will find it so because it is interesting, constructive and amusing, and anyhow I do not think they know the word 'technical'.
The essential point is that parents should be aware that their children need to know more about their bodies in order to understand themselves, their plans and their feelings as well as how new babies are made. If parents can get this across to their children, Claire Rayner's book will do the rest.
This is a book which talks about everything in language which children can understand but with the seriousness as well as the fun that they respect. So many books for children about their bodies miss the point because the author fails to understand what children need. Claire Rayner seems to me to have got the balance exactly right.
I believe that your children will be delighted by this book and that you as parents will enjoy working (playing) with them to help them understand all the important things it explains.

Dr Hugh Jolly

In and   Out.

People are made of food.
Your arms and your legs, your eyes and your
ears, your head and your feet, all grow out
of the food you eat.
So, food works in people the way sun and
water work in flowers in the garden.

People live on food.
To move your arms and your legs, to see
with your eyes and hear with your ears, to
think with your head and skip with your
feet, you need food.
So, food works in people the way petrol
works in cars.

This is how food changes into you.
Take some nuts and raisins.
Your teeth chop them small.
Your tongue stirs them up.
Your spit makes them soft and smooth.
So does drink. Lemonade and orange juice.
Water and milk.
Then, when it is all a nice mush, you
swallow it.

It doesn't just fall down inside you.
It is pushed along a stretchy tube.
The pushing is so strong that even if you
stood on your head to eat your nuts and
raisins, they would still go down into your
stomach.

Your stomach is a soft strong bag which is
just under the edge of your chest, where
your belly begins.
Inside your stomach the nuts and raisins are
made even mushier with special stomach
juices.

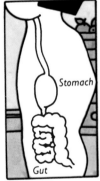

Your stomach stirs up the food by squeezing and squashing it. Put your ear on somebody's belly after they have eaten dinner, and listen. You will hear the squishing and squashing happening.

Burp!

Sometimes when you swallow food you swallow air as well. Then, when your stomach stirs up your food, the air gets pushed back the way it came.
It bubbles back up through the swallowing tube, and comes out through your mouth. This is a burp.

Sometimes a person eats too much and the stomach is too full.

Sometimes a person is ill, and the stomach doesn't want to do the work of stirring up the food.
Then the stomach pushes the food back the way it came, through the swallowing tube, and out through the mouth.
This is being sick.

When the nuts and raisins are all very soft and mixed up they look like thick soup.
Then the stomach pushes it out into your gut, which is also a tube.

Now the food is sorted out. Some of it goes to make new bits of you.

Some of it goes to make your arms and legs work.

Some of it is just no use at all.

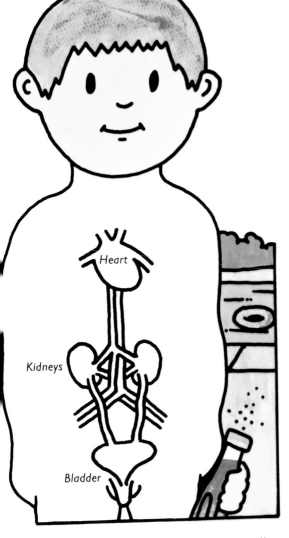

Heart

Kidneys

Bladder

The useful parts are now very, very small. So small they can squeeze through the sides of the tube to get into your blood.

Blood goes all round your body. It carries lots of different things to the different parts of your body.
It carries the useful parts of your nuts and raisins.

But there is still some of the nuts and raisins inside your gut. It is pushed slowly along your gut, down, down, down. Past your belly button.
It is on the way to your bottom.

While it is making its slow journey, some of the water that made the nuts and raisins juicy is squeezed out.

Some of the water is useful, so it goes into the blood. Some of it is not wanted, so it goes to a special part of you called your kidneys.
They are on each side of the bony bit of your back. Kidneys change the water into pee. Its proper name is urine. When your kidneys have made a lot of it, it is kept in a special stretchy bag called your bladder.

It is low down in your belly.

When that is full, you have to go to the lavatory.
And the bag squeezes out the water.

There is still some of the nuts and raisins left inside your gut.
Now it is thick and brown and sticky. It is also a bit smelly, because it is all waste.
As it moves along, sometimes bubbles of air pop up in it. They go all the way to your bottom and push their way out of the little hole there.

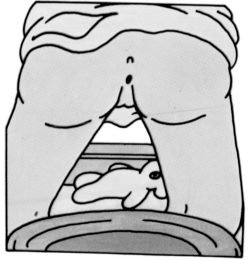

Because the hole is small, the air sometimes makes a funny noise when it comes out. It also makes a smell, because it has been mixed up with the waste.

Pooh!

When the waste reaches the little hole, you have to go to the lavatory again.
Your gut squeezes and squeezes, and pushes out the waste.

Usually it is shaped like the tube it came out of.

Sometimes, if you are not well and your stomach aches, or your gut is in a hurry to get rid of the waste, it comes out all watery.

It takes a whole day for the nuts and raisins to make the journey from your mouth to your bottom.
But you use up so much food for growing and doing, that you want to eat much more often than that.

Isn't it lovely that something as important as eating should also be so much fun?

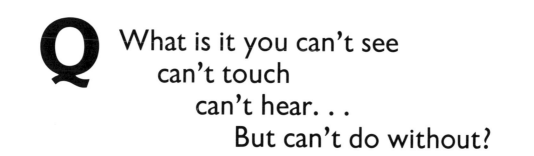

Q What is it you can't see
    can't touch
      can't hear. . .
        But can't do without?

A: Air

Breathing & Talking

Air is as important as food.
It gets into you through your mouth and nose. Inside your nose there are little hairs. They catch any bits of dust and dirt in the air. The bits get mixed up with the slippery wetness which keeps the inside of your nose soft and smooth. They turn into the little black blobs called bogeys.
So, your nose helps to clean the air you breathe.

Sometimes there are germs in the air which make you ill. Inside your nose, right at the back where you can't see them, are the adenoids. They help get rid of the germs that get in.
Inside your mouth at the very back are your tonsils. They help get rid of germs, as well.

Sometimes the tonsils and the adenoids get so filled up with germs that they can't do their job any more. Then the doctor decides to take them out, in a hospital.

The air goes in through your nose and mouth, and down inside your breathing pipe. This leads to your lungs.
They are like sponges, full of tiny holes.
When you breathe in, your chest gets bigger. The holes fill up with air.

Some of your blood travels past the holes, and collects useful clean air from them. Then the air can be carried all over your body. Worn-out air is carried back to your lungs by the blood, and put back in the holes. Then, when you breathe out, your chest gets smaller, and the holes get squashed. So the worn-out air gets pushed out, up into the breathing pipe, and out of your nose and mouth again.

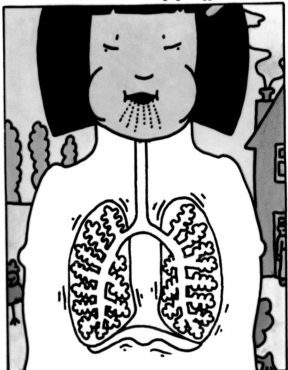

Breathe in . . . lungs get bigger

Breathe out . . . lungs get smaller

7

Sometimes dust and bits from the air get inside your throat and lungs.

Sometimes you catch colds from germs, and then there is a lot of extra slippery stuff inside your nose and throat.

All this gets in the way of the air going in and out. So you have to cough.

First you take a big breath.
Then you breathe out *very* fast, and *very* hard. This blows out the dust or the slippery stuff that was in the way.

It is easy to cough.
You can do it when you like.
But what about sneezing?
You can't make yourself sneeze.

A sneeze happens all by itself when something tickles your nose or throat.
It is also a big breath in, and a fast breath out. But it is *so* big and *so* fast that it blows your nose as well as your throat clear.

Aaa . . .

. . . shoo!

Something else that happens all by itself
is *hiccups!*

These are little jerky breaths that are too
small to let air in and out of your lungs
properly. Usually, if you take no notice of
them, they stop as suddenly as they started.

Hiccup

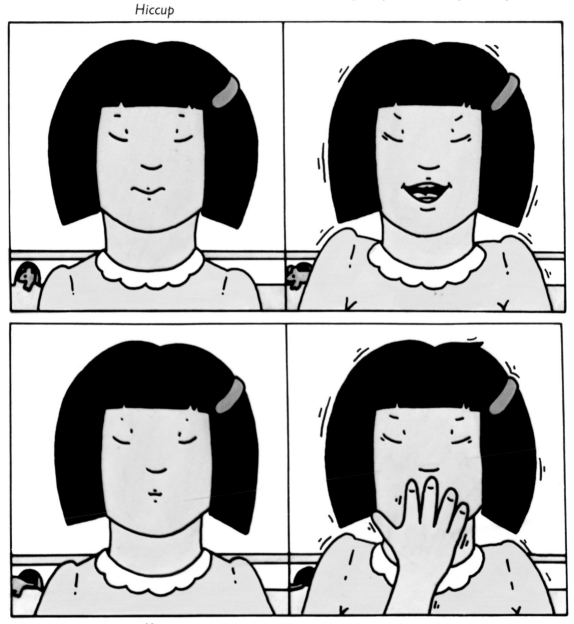

Yawn

9

Sometimes you need some extra air,
because you are tired. Then you take a
huge, slow breath, with your mouth wide
open, to get lots of air in.
This is a yawn.

Sometimes you need a lot of extra air.
Perhaps you have to run to catch a bus.
Then you have to breathe much more
deeply, and much more often.
Afterwards, when you have caught the bus,
you sometimes have to go on breathing
extra fast to make up for all the air you
have used up in running.

Air is needed for lots of things as well as
running.

Like talking.

In your breathing pipe there is a voice box.
Inside it there are two smooth, stretchy
flaps. When air goes over them, they
wobble. This makes them make a sound.
When people talk the flaps stretch in
different ways. This is how they make
different sounds.
How many different sounds can you make
with your voice?

UM
UMMM
UMMMM

A a

Making your mouth into different shapes changes the sounds as well.
How many different sounds can you make with your mouth?

O o

E e

U u

I i

When you use your teeth and your tongue and your lips as well, you can make a lot more interesting sounds. How many interesting sounds can you make with your teeth and tongue and lips?

Ba Ba Ba Ba Ba Ba Ba
Ta Ta Ta Ta Ta Ta Ta
Ss Ss Ss Ss Ss Ss Ss Ss
La La La La La La La La
Da Da Da Da Da Da Da
Mum Mum Mum Mum
Ba Ba Ba Ba Ba Ba Ba
Ta Ta Ta Ta Ta Ta Ta
Ss Ss Ss Ss Ss Ss
La La La La La La
Da Da Da Da
Mum Mum

When you use your throat you can make very good sounds. How many sounds can you make with your throat?

Ka Ka Ka Ka
Ga Ga Ga Ga
Ch Ch Ch Ch

When you have learned how to make all these different sounds, you have learned how to talk.
When you have learned how to make your voice go up and down, you have learned how to sing.
When you have learned to talk so softly that you can hardly hear it, you have learned how to whisper.

Children do not have to learn how to shout.
They are born knowing how.

Some people can whistle.
A lot of people can't.
Whistling is made only with your mouth, not your voice. You make a tiny hole with your lips, and then blow air past your teeth and through the little hole, so that it makes a high noise like a bird.

Blowing out through your lips is very useful. If you make a little hole and blow fast, the air that comes out gets cold.
Also, it can blow away hotness.
This is why you blow on your hot milk to make it cool enough to drink.

If you open your mouth wide, and blow out slowly, the air comes out gently and warmly from inside your warm lungs. This is why you breathe on your hands on a frosty day.

The air breathed out on a frosty day can be seen. It looks like a little white cloud. This is because the air carries some of the wetness from inside your lungs.
This wetness turns into tiny water droplets when the cold air touches it.

Isn't it interesting that something you can't see, can't touch, can't hear, can do so many different things?

13

Beating and Bleeding

You've been beating like a drum since before you were born.

Put your fingers in your ears, shut your eyes tight and listen. You will hear the beating, thump, thump, thump.
The thumping is coming from your heart.
Your heart is inside your chest, in the middle, leaning over sideways a little bit.
Your heart is quite big. It is as big as your clenched fist. A grown-up's heart is as big as his clenched fist. Everyone has the right-sized heart for his body.
Your heart beats because it is a pump.
It keeps pushing your blood around your body.
It works all day and all night.
It never stops.
Push, rest, push, rest, push, rest.
Thump, thump, thump.
How does it push the blood where it has to go?

Joined to your heart there are some very thick tubes.
They are joined to thinner ones.
They are joined to even thinner ones.
Then there are some very, *very* thin ones.
They are joined to some more very, very thin ones.
Then there are some thicker ones.
Then there are some very thick ones.
And they join up with your heart again.

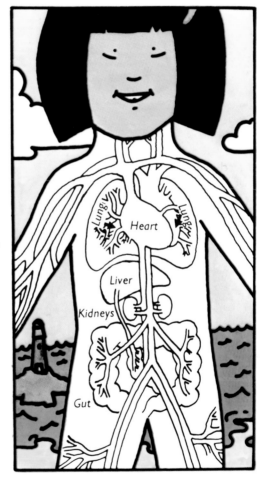

14

So your blood goes round and round in a big circle, all the time. Sometimes you can see this happen on a person's wrist. Not your own, because children's blood tubes are hard to see.

Look at a grown-up's wrist. You will see blue lines. These are blood tubes called veins. Stroke one with your finger, downwards towards the hand.

See the blueness go away? That is the blood. Now let go. See the blueness come back? The heart-beat has pushed it back. That is how the blood gets to every part of your body. It must do that, because it is the blood which carries all the different things your body parts need.

When your ears need some food and air to help them listen, the blood carries it to them. When your big toe needs some food and air to help it waggle, your blood carries it there.

White cell

Red cell

Blood does other things as well.
It takes care of you. Suppose some germs
get into your body? They sometimes do,
because there are lots of germs about.

In the blood are some
germ-fighters. They go to
the place where the germs
are getting in, and they swallow
them up.
Just . . . . . like . . . . . that!
Your blood also carries mending stuff.
When you cut yourself, some of the
blood gets out of the tubes. This is a
nuisance because it makes your clothes
all bloody.

It is also a waste, because blood is so useful.
So, little bits of the blood join together and
make a plug for the hole.
It is called a clot.
The clot gets thicker, and tighter and harder.
Underneath, the cut starts to join together
again. When it is all joined up, the hard
dry clot falls off.
You are mended.

Some people are frightened of blood.
Isn't that silly, when blood is so useful and
interesting?

16

Running, Jumping and

Standing Still

Skeletons aren't scary.
There is one inside you.
Hold your finger gently. It will feel soft.
Now hold it more tightly. It will feel hard.
The hard bit is a bone.
You have more than two hundred bones
in your body.
Some are very long and thick. The ones in
your legs, from your bottom to your knees,
are long and thick.
Some are very small and thin. The ones in
the tips of your smallest toes are small
and thin.

Some don't look like bones at all.
Look inside your mouth.
Can you see your teeth?
They are a sort of bone.

Why do you have bones?
To help you stand up.
If you didn't have bones, you'd be as
floppy as a jelly.

Why do you have so many?
So that you can move about.
If you had just one big bone that filled all
of you, you'd be as stiff as a scarecrow.

Having lots of little bones all joined together
means you can walk and skip and dance.
It means your fingers can do up buttons.
It means your toes can wriggle.

Your bones are joined together with thick,
flat, stretchy bands, like rubber bands.

They make different sorts of joins between
the bones.
Some joins let the bones go round and
round. Your shoulder has that sort of join.
Some joins let the bones move in one
way only. Your knee has that sort of join.
Some joins let the bones slide over

each other. Your wrist has that sort of join.

There are some very special bones in your
back. They are all joined together so that
you can bend forwards . . .
    and sideways . . .
        and a little bit backwards.

The bones don't move by
themselves. They need muscles
to move them.

There are more than six hundred
different muscles in your body.

Back bones

18

Pinch your arm, and pinch your leg.
The thick softness you can feel under your
skin is muscles. They are very remarkable.
They can make themselves short and thick.
And then they can make themselves long
and flat again.
Hold out your arm, straight out.
Put your other hand over the top part of it.
Now, make your elbow bend.
Feel how the muscle in the top of your arm
gets thicker and shorter. It is pulling up the
bone in the front of your arm.
When a muscle gets short and thick, it is
like a storehouse. It is a storehouse full
of work.

When it goes thinner and flatter, then it is
sending out its work. The work can take
you up the stairs, or push your bicycle
along.
That is hard work. It is so hard it
makes you feel warm.

But muscles do other work as well.
There are tiny muscles which make
your eyes move, and your tongue
talk.

This is not hard work, but it is very
complicated work. And muscles do it
very well.

Bones and muscles together work
very hard for you.

19

Tasting, Smelling, Seeing, Hearing and Touching.

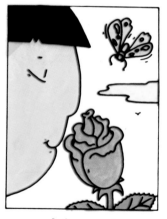

Mmm!

Pooh!

Yum!

You can find out more than detectives can, just using bits of your own body. You can find out if food is good to eat, just by smelling it. If the food is bad, it will smell bad, and your nose will tell you so.

Smells travel in the air, and go into your nose when you breathe.
You can't see smells.
They are like air, quite invisible.
Inside your nose are special smell-collectors.
They send the smell along a pathway called a nerve.
The nerve goes to your brain.

Your brain thinks about the smell.
If it is a good food smell, your brain makes you feel hungry. Your mouth fills with spit, ready to eat the good smelling food.

If it is a smell of the scent your mother uses, your brain makes you feel happy, if your mother is with you.
Or a little bit lonely if she is not.

If it is a bad smell your brain makes you move your nose away from it. It tells you to wrinkle your nose, or cover it with your hand. It sometimes makes you try to blow away the air which has the bad smell in it.
That is why people say 'Pooh!' to bad smells.
It is a blowing-away sort of word.

Smells and tastes go together.
If something smells good enough to eat, it usually tastes good as well.
If you can't smell what you are eating, it doesn't taste so good. This is because smell-nerves and taste-nerves like to work together.

Taste starts in your tongue.
The very tip of your tongue collects sweet tastes.
Like honey.

The middle and sides of your tongue collect
sour tastes.
Like lemon slices.
The back of your tongue collects bitter
tastes.
Like the black chocolate that grown-ups eat.

When you are little you usually like the
tip-of-your-tongue tastes most.
Grown-ups often like the middle- and
back-of-the-tongue tastes most.

Your nose collects smells.
Your tongue collects tastes.
What do your eyes collect?

Light.

22

They collect it through a little window in the middle of your eye. If the light is very bright the little window closes itself a bit. If the light is very low, the little window widens itself a bit.

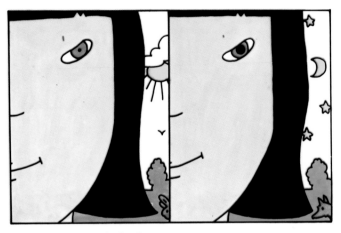

Stand in a dim, dark place.
Look at your eyes in a mirror. See how wide open the little window is. Now move to a brighter, sunnier place. See how the little windows get smaller.

Eyes are very clever.
They can collect all the different light and shade patterns, all the different colour patterns, all the different shape patterns.

But they do it in a very funny way. They collect it all upside down!

This is how the picture you are looking at is inside your eye.

This is how the picture you are looking at is inside your brain.
It is your brain which turns the picture the right way up.

Your ears collect sounds.
Sound is made by wobbles in the air.
The wobbles are called vibrations.
The vibrations go first into the outside part
of your ear.

Then, they go into the hole in your ear.

At the other end of the hole is a smooth,
flat piece of skin, just like the cover on
a drum.

When the vibrations touch it, it wobbles as
well. Then the vibrations go deeper inside
your ear, making some tiny bones wobble.

And then, at last, the vibrations get to your
brain, and your brain knows that they are
sounds.

Ears and eyes like to work together.
It is easier to hear what someone is saying
if you can watch their lips move.

All of your body collects touch feelings.

You can use your arms or your legs, your feet or your knees or your bottom, to find out if things are hot or cold or hard or soft.

But some bits of your body are much better than others at finding out.

Like your finger-tips, and the tip of your tongue. Babies like feeling things with their tongues best of all. That is why they put everything into their mouths.

A very soft touch feels like a tickle. A very hard touch feels like a pain.

Most people don't like pains, but they are very useful.

Suppose you could put your hand in a fire and not feel it? Then you would not take your hand away, and you would burn it very badly.

Because it hurts, you take your hand away very quickly. And then your hand is safe.

Pains are very useful, because they find out about danger and warn us.

All of your body is good at finding out things.

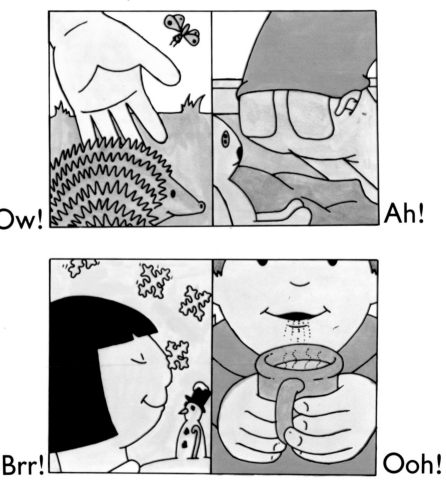

Ow!

Ah!

Brr!

Ooh!

Thinking and Feeling.

The most exciting things in the world happen inside your head.
This is where your brain is.
Your brain has a lot of work to do.

It looks after your body.
It tells it how to work.

It tells your stomach to squeeze and squash your food.
It tells your heart to beat like a drum.
It tells you how to run and how to jump and how to stand still.

How does your brain look after your body?

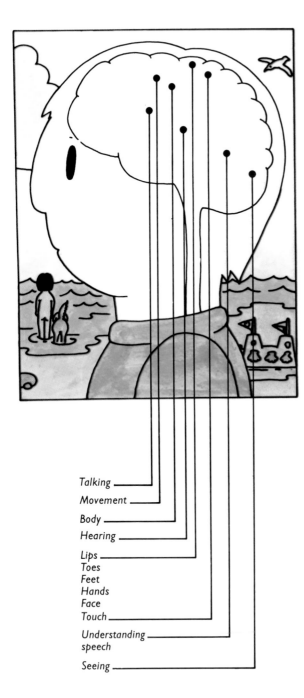

Talking
Movement
Body
Hearing
Lips
Toes
Feet
Hands
Face
Touch
Understanding
speech
Seeing

Inside your brain are lots and lots of little pathways. The pathways lead out of your brain and go all over your body. Your brain sends its messages along the pathways.

The different parts of your body use the pathways as well. They send messages back to the brain along them. That is how your brain knows what is happening to every bit of your body.
Take off your shoe and sock.
At once your foot sends a message to your brain.
"I'm getting cold," it says.
Your brain sends a message to your hands.
"Put the sock and shoe back on. Your foot is cold," it says.

Then your brain sends messages to the muscles of your hands about how to put the sock and shoe back on.

Your brain also thinks and feels.

Thinking is a lot of different things.
Thinking is remembering.
When you make a house of bricks, your brain remembers how you did it last time.
Thinking is inventing new ways of doing things.
When you want to make a different sort of house of bricks, your brain invents the new way.
Thinking is working out things.
When you haven't enough bricks to make the house you want, your brain works out different ways to use the bricks you've got.

Feeling is also a lot of different things.
Feeling is being happy because you are doing what you want to do. Happy feelings make you want to laugh.
Feeling is being angry because someone won't let you do what you want to do. Angry feelings make you want to shout and stamp.

Feeling is being frightened because someone
you need isn't there. Frightened feelings
make you want to cry.

You can make feelings happen by thinking
about them.

Hungry   *Frightened*

Make a picture of yourself inside your head.
See yourself come home from playing.
You are hungry.
Think about how hungry you are.
Can you feel your empty stomach?
Can you feel your mouth filling up with spit,
ready for food you will have?

Now make a picture of you in your house.
Your mother isn't there.
Where is she?
Look for her.
The rooms are quiet and empty.
You begin to be frightened.

Feel the fright inside you.
Your stomach feels full of cold.
Your knees feel wobbly.
All of you is filled up with frightened
feelings because your mother isn't there.

Relieved   *Angry*   *Happy*

Now, change the picture in your head.
Your mother is coming in.

She only went next door for a moment.
She didn't mean to frighten you.

How do you feel now?

Can you feel the angry feelings coming into you?
She was very naughty to go out and leave you to be frightened.

You are very, very angry.
You stamp your feet and shout at her.
You feel horrible.

Make the picture of your mother cuddle you and kiss you and say she is sorry.
Now can you feel the happy loving feelings coming back? She is here and you are safe.
It is a good feeling.

Your brain made all these feelings happen.
Just by thinking about them.

Even when you're tired and fast asleep, your brain still goes on working. It makes night-time pictures in your head.
These are dreams.
A brain is a very exciting thing to have.

29

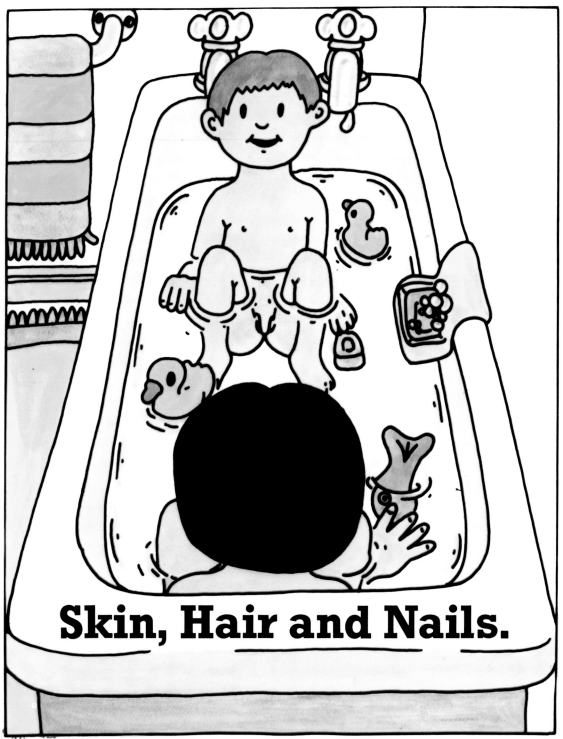

Skin, Hair and Nails.

What is the biggest part of your whole body?
Your skin.
It covers every bit of you.

It protects you from germs.
Germs can't get into your body through
your skin unless there is a cut in it.
It keeps all the important parts inside you
safe and comfortable.

There is a lot of water in your inside parts
and if you did not have a nice thick
protecting skin the water would all get out.
And then you would be as dried up and
hard and wrinkled as an old bean.

It stops water from outside getting in.
If too much got in, from the rain or from
your bath, you would be as soggy as a wet
sponge.

Your skin looks after itself as well as you.
It needs to be smooth and soft and stretchy.
So, it makes smoothing, softening oil in
special little holes in itself.

Look at your skin through a magnifying glass.
You will be able to see the holes. This oil
spreads very thinly all over your skin.
It catches dirt and dust in it.
That is why you have to wash so often.
When you have washed off the dirty old oil,
new oil is made.

Hairs grow in your skin, all over you, except
on the soles of your feet and on the palms of
your hands. In some parts of you the hair is
very thick and easy to see.
Like on your head.

In other places it is so soft and short you
have to look very closely for it.
Like on your arms and legs.

Why is the hair there on your body?
It is a left over!
Millions and millions of years ago, human
beings were more like animals than people.
They had thick hairy coats on their skins.
Then gradually people got smoother and
smoother. Each baby born had less hair than
its mother and father.
Nowadays most people have only little bits
of left-over hair on their bodies.
But . . .

They still have the little muscles that can lift
up each hair.
Animals need to do this.

When a furry cat is cold, she makes each hair
stand up on end. This helps keep warm air
close to her body and makes her feel warmer.

When a furry dog is frightened of another
animal, he makes each hair stand up on end.
This makes him look much bigger and fiercer,
and frightens away the animal he is afraid of.

This is why when people are cold or
frightened they get little bumps called
gooseflesh all over them. Their skin has
remembered that once, millions of years ago,
people did what furry animals do.
And it still makes it happen.

Skin comes in lots of different colours. It can
be almost white or pale pink or beige or
cream or chocolate or shiny black.

Why does skin come in different colours?

32

It is all because of the sun.
When very hot sun shines on people's pale skins, it can hurt them and burn them.
So, skin makes itself a protection.
It makes itself go brown.
This is called a tan.

Some people get only little patches of tan.
They are called freckles.

Millions and millions of years ago, when people first started being people and stopped being animals, they lived in different parts of the world.
They did not travel.
They stayed in the same places all the time.

Some parts of the world were very, very hot, with burning sunshine.
Some were very, very cool, with hardly any sunshine.
And there were all sorts of places in between, with medium sunshine.

The people who lived in the very hot sunshiny places got very dark tans. Only the ones who had skins which could get very brown or black could live there. They were the only ones who grew up and had babies.
So, black and very dark brown people started out in the hot places of the world.

The people who lived in very cool places did not get brown at all. They all grew up and had babies as pale as themselves.
So, pale people started out in the cold places of the world.

And in-between coloured people came from the in-between places.

Nowadays people travel about the world a lot and like to live in different places.
That is why you find pale people and black people and brown people all living together in different parts of the world.

33

Look at the ends of your fingers and toes.
The nails that are there are not made of
metal, like the nails that you hammer into
wood. They are made of skin!

Skin can go very hard, and make itself
very strong.
Then it can be used to do work.

Finger nails are useful for all sorts of work,
like cutting and scraping and digging.
In the long ago times before people's brains
had invented tools like knives and spades,
they only had their nails to do work with.

That is why we still have nails.
They are left-overs from the olden days,
like the hair on our arms.

Toe nails are left-overs too, from the days
when people had feet as useful as their
hands are.
Look at the monkeys in the zoo next time
you go.
They have feet like hands.

So did we, once, millions of years before
you were born.

Growing and Changing and Making New People.

Children are the fathers and mothers of grown-ups.
That sounds silly, doesn't it?
What does it really mean?
It means that children grow and change until one day they are grown-ups themselves, and then they can make babies.

How do children grow into grown-ups who can make babies?

First of all their bodies have to grow. Their bones must get thicker, their muscles stronger, their hearts bigger, and their arms and legs longer.

36

How does this happen?
All your bones and muscles and every part
of you are made of tiny building pieces,
called cells. When cells get all the food and
air they need from the blood, they grow
and grow.
Soon they are twice as big as they were.
Then, they split in half and become two
separate building pieces. The two grow and
grow and become four cells. Then the four
become eight, and the eight sixteen.
And on and on and on, until the little child
is almost a grown-up person.

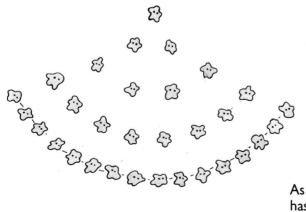

That is how each bit of you gets bigger,
and makes the whole of you bigger.

When boys and girls are almost grown-up,
some important bits of them start to grow.
These are the baby-making bits.

Inside her belly, deep down and safely
tucked away, a girl has a storehouse of tiny
baby-making cells. When she is a woman,
they can grow into babies.

But they can't grow into babies by
themselves.
They have to join with a special seed from
a man before they can do that.

As well as the baby-making eggs, a woman
has a place inside her where a baby can grow.

She also grows big, round, soft breasts
on the front of her chest.
They are for making milk to feed a baby with.
They are also to help her cuddle her baby.
Being cuddled by a mother with warm soft
breasts is very nice for babies and children.

Boys have baby-making bits as well.
They have little round balls where
baby-making seeds grow.
They are in between their legs.
They get bigger when the boy grows up.

Boys also have a penis, which they use to
pee with.
This gets bigger as well.

37

It will have another job to do when the boy is a man. It will have the job of putting the baby-making seeds deep inside the woman's baby-making place, so that the egg and seed together can grow into a baby.

This is how it happens.

When a man and a woman want to make a baby, the man's penis stops being floppy and hanging down.
It stands to attention.

This is a special grown-up way of loving someone very much. It is the most loving sort of cuddle there is for grown-ups.

The seeds come out of the man's penis and go to meet the woman's baby-making egg. The man's seeds are called sperm, and they can swim.
They have whippy little tails to help them. When a sperm meets the egg, they join together and start to grow and change. It takes a long, long time.

Then he can put it gently inside the woman's baby-making hole.

38

Almost as long as it is from one of your birthdays to the next one.

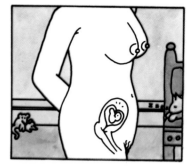

The baby grows bigger . . .

. . . and bigger . . .

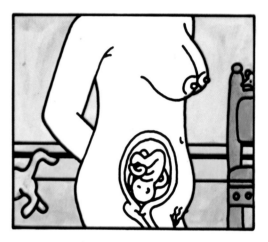

. . . and bigger

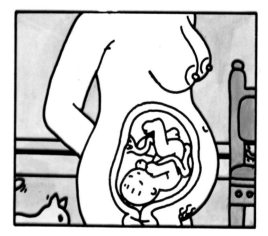

Until at last he is big enough to live outside his mother's body, by himself.

It is hard work for a mother to help her baby get out.
She has to stretch her baby-making place very wide, and that takes a lot of time.
But it is worth the hard work, because a new baby is a very happy person to have in a family.

After the baby is born, his mother holds him close to her breasts and puts the soft tip of one of them in his mouth. Then he can suck, and get out the milk the breasts are making.

Yum!

Mothers like doing this.
It feels nice for them.
Babies like doing this.
It feels nice for them, too.

Because the new baby is made of a little
bit of his mother, and a little bit of his father,
he is a mixture of both of them.
Even a boy is half like his mother.
Even a girl is half like her father.
And because mothers and fathers are each
like *their* mothers and fathers, a new baby is
a quarter of each of his grandparents!

He may have the same shaped nose as one
grandmother, and the same coloured eyes as
the other one. He may have curly hair like
his father, or brown hair like his mother.

Look at your mother and father and at your
grandmothers and grandfathers, if you can,
and see which bits of them match bits of you.

One day you will make babies as well,
and they will look like you, and like your
mother and father, and like your
grandparents, and even your great
grandparents.

And one day you will be a grandparent
yourself.

Fancy that.

Growing Old and Dying.

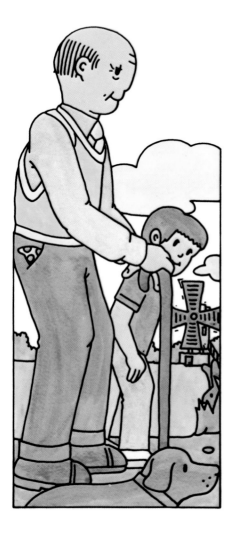

Nobody and nothing lasts for ever.
Flowers start by being little seeds,
and then turn into shoots and then grow
buds which turn into flowers. Then the
flower droops and the petals drop off,
the leaves wither and the plant dies.
But the seeds it made start growing all
over again.

People start by being little seeds.
Then they grow into babies, and the babies
grow into children, and the children
grow into grown-ups.
Then they make new people.
Do they stop growing after they have
grown up and made new people?
They stop growing, but they don't stop
changing.

Old people are different from young ones.
Their muscles are not so good at storing
up work. So, old people have to walk
slower and sometimes have to use a stick
to help their muscles hold them up.

Their skin is not so good at smoothing
itself, so it gets wrinkled.

Their hair is not so good at growing, so it gets thin and loses its colour.
Sometimes it stops growing altogether!

Sometimes their ears are not so good at hearing, so people have to talk louder for them.

Their brains are still as good at thinking and feeling and sending messages, but they get tired more quickly.
So, old people like to take naps in the daytime, to help their brains rest after doing all their work.

After many, many years, long after their children are grown up, people who are old get tired all over.
Their hearts get tired of beating like a drum.
Their muscles get tired of storing up work.
Their brains get tired of thinking and feeling.
The time has come for the old person to die.

So they do.

All their different body parts quietly stop working. They cannot see or feel or think or be busy any more.

It is a very peaceful way to be.

Sometimes people get very ill and their bodies get tired enough to die, before they are old. Sometimes even babies die.
But that is unusual.
Usually it is old people who die.

Usually when a person dies, all the people in the family are sad. They will miss having the person to talk to, and be with.
So they cry.
Grown-ups can cry just as children can.

After a person has died, they don't need their tired, worn-out body any more.
So, they are buried in the soft earth.
Everyone in the family goes to say goodbye to the dead body being put in the earth.

This is a funeral.

At the funeral people put flowers on the place where the dead person is buried.
They are a goodbye present.
Slowly, the flowers die too.
They droop and go brown and crumble away. The different tiny parts of the flowers and their leaves mix up with the earth, and turn into new earth.

The same thing happens to the dead person.

They turn into new earth as well.

New earth is needed to grow flowers and vegetables and grass to feed animals.
Animals are needed to make milk and eggs to go with the vegetables that grew in the earth.
All these different foods come from the earth. Which is very useful because people are made of food!

So, dead people become part of new people in a very helpful way.

That is not the only way in which dead people are part of new people.

Their feelings and their memories can become part of a child's feelings and memories.

Many of the things you learn from your mother and father, they learned from their mother and father, who were your grandparents.

And the things your grandparents learned from their mother and father came from *their* grandparents.

One day, when you are grown up and have children, you will teach them the things you have learned. And your children will grow up and teach their children, who will be your grandchildren, the things *they* have learned.

Which means that many of the things you learn now, and feel now and know now, have come from long ago, and will go on for years and years.

So, although nobody and nothing lasts for ever – everybody does!

Scholastic Children's Books
Commonwealth House, 1-19 New Oxford Street
London WC1A 1NU, UK
a division of Scholastic Ltd
London ~ New York ~ Toronto ~ Sydney ~ Auckland
Mexico City ~ New Delhi ~ Hong Kong

First published by G. Whizzard Publications Ltd in association with André Deutsch, 1978
First published in paperback by Pan Books Ltd, 1979
This edition first published in paperback by Scholastic Ltd, 1994

ISBN 0 590 55608 8

Printed in Italy by Amadeus S.p.A. – Rome

10 12 14 16 18 20 19 17 15 13 11 9